indian

Written by Harmeet Hooren-Sagoo

imagine **THAT!**™

Imagine That! is an imprint of Top That! Publishing plc,
Tide Mill Way, Woodbridge, Suffolk, IP12 IAP, UK
www.topthatpublishing.com
Copyright © 2010 Top That! Publishing plc
Imagine That! is a trademark of Top That! Publishing plc.

Contents

Contents

Topham Picturepoint

Indian cuisine is becoming more and more popular worldwide. The range of dishes – often just called 'curry' as a general catch-all – forms the staple diet of the Indian subcontinent.

The term 'curry' was adopted by the British Raj in the 19th century and became known in the West as the general expression for Indian cuisine. However, in Indian households curry isn't a word that is widely used, and instead the individual dishes are called by their Indian names.

The ingredients and character of the dishes vary depending on the region from which they originate.

North western India is predominantly a wheat-growing region and so Indian breads, such as chapatti (roti) and paranthas, form part of the staple diet. A curry here consists of a 'tarka' – a basic gravy used as the basis for a dish consisting of a mixture of cooked onions, garlic, ginger and spices (usually chilli, salt, turmeric and tomatoes). In the southern regions rice is grown, therefore rice dishes dominate the cuisine. Fish and seafood are also very popular.

There is a wide selection of vegetarian dishes in Indian cuisine. Indeed, the state of Gujarat, in west India, follows a strict vegetarian diet.

The spiciness of a curry depends on the amount of chilli used in the dish. Curries do not have to be hot.

Removing the seeds from the chillies or adding cream or coconut milk will make a curry milder. For example, a Korma is a very mild and thick sauce cooked with cream and fresh herbs. A madras curry, which originates from Madras in India is a fairly hot curry cooked in a rich sauce. The hottest curry dishes available are vindaloo or phall dishes.

The Indian subcontinent contains many different cultures and religions including Hindus, Sikhs, Christians and Muslims. This has influenced the development of Indian cuisine. For example, the cow is sacred in India and so beef curries are almost never found. The meat used is either mutton, lamb, chicken or goat.

Cow's milk, however, is used in many different ways in Indian cuisine. It is used to make yoghurts and curds such as Indian cheese – paneer (see page 9).

Milk is also used to make the popular Indian beverage, 'lassi' (see page 93). In the West, beer is the traditional accompaniment to curry and there are a number of Indian beers such as Cobra lager and Kingfisher. However, in India it is lassi – a yoghurt-based drink – that is traditionally drunk with a curry.

Whether you are looking to create an authentic taste of India, or simply wishing to broaden your culinary skills, this book will give you new ideas, techniques and recipes that will really spice up your kitchen.

Basic Equipment

Heavy-based saucepan
Frying pan
Karahi (double handled 'wok'-style cooking and serving bowl)
Rolling pin
Metal slotted or perforated spoon
Clean tea towels
Wooden spoons
Weighing scales
Measuring jug
Sieve
Muslin cloths

The preparation and cooking times in these recipes are approximate and will depend upon whether you are using gas or electricity, and how familiar you are with the recipes.

Imperial weight conversions are approximate. For best results use either metric or imperial measurements throughout the recipe.

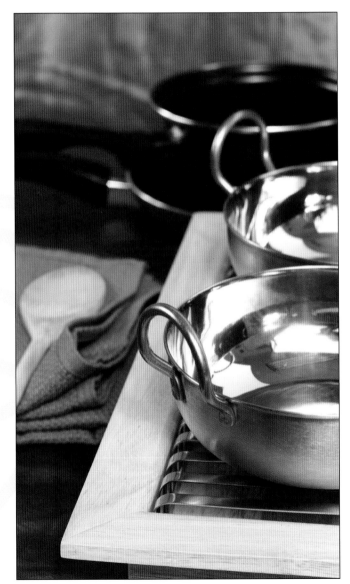

Basic Ingredients

The spices and ingredients used in this book can be bought from your local Indian grocers or may be available from supermarkets. Most of the spices used are ground spices that can be bought in packets. When using fresh green chillies in these recipes you can decide whether to deseed the chilli or not. The curry will be hotter if you leave the seeds in.

Garam Masala

Garam masala – a blend of spices – is particularly important and is used in most curries. You can buy pre-packed garam masala or mix the spices yourself as follows:

50 g (2 oz) cinnamon
50 g (2 oz) cloves
50 g (2 oz) white cumin seeds
50 g (2 oz) coriander seeds
50 g (2 oz) black cardamom seeds
50 g (2 oz) black peppercorns (optional)

Basic Ingredients

Ghee (clarified butter)

Ghee is another important component of Indian cuisine. For a truly authentic taste you can use the following recipe. However, this is not absolutely essential; the more health-conscious cook can substitute olive, vegetable or sunflower oil in recipes that call for ghee.

- 250 g (9 oz) butter
- 1 tsp lemon juice
- medium-sized jar

1. Place the butter in a saucepan on a low heat. Heat the butter until melted.

2. Add the lemon juice and simmer for 10 minutes. The butter will separate and the fat will be left at the bottom. The ghee will remain on the top.

3. Strain the mixture in a sieve, discarding the bottom layer, and transfer the ghee to a jar to set.

Homemade yoghurt (Dahi)

This is used in Indian cuisine to cool the spiciness of a dish, and is also the chief ingredient of raita (page 77).

- 560 ml (20 fl oz) milk – full fat or semi-skimmed
- 1 tsp plain yoghurt

1. Boil the milk in a pan and then leave to cool. When it is lukewarm, place the milk in an insulated dish. If an insulated dish isn't available, then place in a normal dish in a warm place covered tightly with a cloth.

2. Add the yoghurt. Leave for 5 hours or overnight to set.

Basic Ingredients

Paneer — Indian cheese

This forms the basis of Saag Paneer (page 35).

- 2.3 litres (4 pts) full fat milk
- 2–3 tbsp white wine vinegar
- muslin cloth

I. In a pan, boil the milk over a medium heat, being careful not to burn it.

2. Once boiled, add the vinegar to curdle the milk. Remove from the heat.

3. Place a muslin cloth in a sieve or colander and strain the milk mixture. You will be left with the curds, or paneer.

4. Wrap up the paneer in the cloth and place a weight on top of the cloth. Leave for 15 minutes.

5. The paneer can then be cut into chunks or used loose – it needs to be lightly fried before use.

Chicken Tikka Masala

Chicken Tikka Masala

You will need:

Chicken Marinade

- 1 tsp grated ginger
- 1 tsp grated garlic
- 1 tsp ground coriander
- 1 tsp ground cumin
- 1 tsp chilli powder
- 6 tbsp natural yoghurt
- 1 tsp salt
- 2 tbsp lemon juice
- 1 tsp tomato purée
- 1 tsp turmeric
- 1 tsp paprika
- 1 tsp chicken tikka masala powder
- 900 g (2 lb) chicken breast (cubed)
- 1 medium onion, chopped

Sauce

- 100 g (4 oz) raw cashew nuts
- 200 ml (7 fl.oz) double cream
- 800 g (1 lb, 12 oz) tinned tomatoes, chopped
- 1 tbsp tomato purée
- 3 tsp sugar
- 1 tsp salt
- 2 tsp white cumin seeds
- 1 tsp chilli powder
- 1 tsp garam masala
- 1 large knob of butter
- a bunch fresh coriander

Preparation time: 8–10 minutes
Cooking time: 1 hour 10 minutes
Marinating time: 3 hours minimum (preferably overnight)
Serves: 6

Chicken Tikka Masala

For the chicken

1. Place the ginger, garlic, coriander, cumin and chilli powder in a mixing bowl and blend together.

2. Add the yoghurt, salt, lemon juice, tomato purée, turmeric, paprika and chicken tikka masala powder.

3. Cut the chicken into small pieces and add to the spice and yoghurt mixture. Marinate the chicken for at least 3 hours or overnight.

4. Place the chopped onions in the bottom of a baking tray or glass heatproof dish.

5. Preheat the oven to 200°C/400°F/gas mark 6 and place the marinated chicken pieces on top of the onions and cook for 40–45 minutes, turning over occasionally. While the chicken is cooking prepare the sauce. Alternatively, serve the chicken without the sauce for classic chicken tikka.

For the sauce

1. Place the cashew nuts into a blender and blend for a few seconds. Add half the cream.

2. Place the mixture in a pan with the tinned tomatoes, tomato purée, sugar, salt, cumin seeds, chilli powder and garam masala. Simmer for 25 minutes, adding a little water if necessary. Stir the mixture occasionally to prevent it from sticking.

3. Add the cooked chicken tikka to the sauce and stir in the butter, the remaining cream and the coriander. Taste the sauce and check the seasoning, adding more salt or chilli if required. Serve garnished with more fresh coriander if desired.

Chicken Korma

Chicken Korma

You will need:

- 25 g (1 oz) flaked almonds
- 1 tsp ginger, grated
- 1 tsp garlic, grated
- 1 tsp white cumin seeds
- 1 tsp ground coriander
- 1 tsp paprika
- ½ tsp chilli powder
- 4 tbsp natural yoghurt
- 4 chicken breasts
- 3 tbsp oil
- 1 medium onion, finely chopped
- ½ tsp salt
- 1 tbsp lemon juice
- 200 ml (7 fl.oz) water
- 150 ml (5 fl.oz) double cream
- 1 tsp sugar
- 2 tbsp coconut milk
- handful fresh coriander, chopped
- 1 tsp garam masala

Preparation time: 5–10 minutes
Cooking time: 50–55 minutes
Marinating time: 15–20 minutes
Serves: 4

1. Roast the almonds on a baking tray in a hot oven for a few minutes. Mix the ginger, garlic, white cumin seeds, ground coriander, paprika, chilli powder with the almonds and the yoghurt.

2. Marinate chicken in the yoghurt and spice mixture for 15–20 minutes.

3. Heat the oil in a pan. Add the onion and cook until golden brown.

4. Add the marinated chicken pieces, the salt and lemon juice and cook for 5–7 minutes.

5. Add the water, cover and simmer for 10 minutes, stirring occasionally, before adding the cream.

6. Simmer for another 10 minutes, then add the sugar, coconut milk, fresh coriander and garam masala and cook for a further 3–4 minutes, stirring occasionally.

7. Serve with boiled rice and garnish with more flaked almonds.

Chicken Vindaloo

Chicken Vindaloo

You will need:

- 1 tsp ground coriander
- 1 tsp white cumin seeds
- 4 whole cloves
- 5 cm (2 in.) cinnamon stick
- 2 tsp black peppercorns
- 1 tsp ground fenugreek
- 60 ml (2 fl.oz) white vinegar
- 1 kg (2 lb, 3 oz) chicken (boneless)
- 3 tbsp ghee / oil
- 6 garlic cloves, peeled and finely chopped
- 1 large onion chopped
- 2 tsp ginger, finely grated
- 3 tsp tomato paste
- 1 tsp salt
- 6 dried red or green chillies
- ½ tsp chilli powder
- 2 curry leaves
- 425 ml (15 fl.oz) water
- 2 tbsp yoghurt
- ½ –1 tsp tandoori powder
- fresh coriander

Preparation time: 5–10 minutes
Cooking time: 30–40 minutes
Marinating time: 5–8 minutes
Serves: 4–6

1. Grind all of the spices in a pestle and mortar and dry fry in a pan on a medium heat for 30 seconds, then mix with the vinegar.

2. Cut the chicken into cubes and coat with the spice mixture. Leave to saturate for 5–8 minutes.

3. Heat the ghee / oil in a saucepan and sauté the meat until it is evenly coloured.

4. Finely chop the garlic, onion and ginger and add to the pan. Cook for 5–8 minutes until the onions are soft, then add the tomato paste, salt, dried chillies and chilli powder. Cook for 2–3 minutes.

5. Add the curry leaves and water, cover and cook on a moderate heat for 15–20 minutes, stirring occasionally. Then remove the lid, add the yoghurt and tandoori powder and cook for a further 2–3 minutes, until the sauce thickens slightly.

6. Garnish with fresh coriander leaves if desired.

Tandoori Chicken

Tandoori Chicken

You will need:
- 8 chicken drumsticks or 400 g (14 oz) chicken pieces
- 4 tbsp yoghurt
- 1 ½ tsp fresh garlic, peeled and crushed
- 1 ½ tsp fresh ginger, grated
- 1 ½ tsp chilli powder
- 1 tsp ground cumin
- 1 tsp ground coriander
- 1 tbsp lemon juice
- ½ tsp salt
- 1 tbsp tandoori powder
- Garnish with: lettuce leaves, onions, sliced tomatoes and lemon wedges

Preparation time: 5–8 minutes
Cooking time: 1 hour
Marinating time: 4 hours minimum (preferably overnight)
Serves: 4

1. Make 2–3 slashes in each chicken drumstick so they can absorb the spices.

2. Place the yoghurt, garlic, ginger, chilli powder, ground cumin, ground coriander, lemon juice, salt and tandoori powder in a bowl and mix together.

3. Add the chicken to the mixture and stir in thoroughly. Leave to marinate in the fridge for a minimum of 4 hours, or overnight.

4. Preheat the oven to 200°C/400°F/gas mark 6. Place the chicken in a heatproof dish. Cook for 45–55 minutes, turning the chicken pieces occasionally to prevent them burning.

5. Serve on a bed of lettuce and garnish with onion rings, sliced tomatoes and lemon wedges.

Lamb Curry

Lamb Curry

You will need:

- 2–3 tbsp ghee / oil
- 1 medium onion, chopped
- 1 tsp fresh garlic, grated
- 1 tsp fresh ginger, grated
- 500 g (17½ oz) lamb pieces
- 1 tsp turmeric
- 1 tsp salt
- 1 tsp chilli powder
- 1 tsp white cumin seeds
- 150 g (5 oz) tinned tomatoes
- 2 tbsp natural yoghurt
- 2 tbsp lemon juice
- 1 tsp meat masala (optional)
- 600 ml (20 fl.oz) water
- 1 tsp garam masala
- handful of fresh coriander, chopped

Note: *Meat masala is a spice mixture that can be purchased as a pre-prepared mix.*

Preparation time: 6–10 minutes
Cooking time: 1 hour 30 minutes
Serves: 4

1. Heat the ghee / oil in a pan. Sauté the onions, garlic and ginger and stir-fry for 2–3 minutes. Add the lamb pieces, cover and cook for 10–15 minutes on a moderate / low heat, stirring occasionally.

2. Remove the lid and cook for a further 10 minutes.

3. Add turmeric, salt, chilli powder, cumin and tomatoes and cook for 2–3 minutes. Add the yoghurt, lemon juice and meat masala (if using). Cook for 25–35 minutes on a moderate heat until the lamb is tender. Stir occasionally.

4. Add the water and cook for a further 30–40 minutes on a low heat until the liquid has halved and you are left with a thicker sauce. Finally, add the garam masala and fresh coriander and cook for a final 2 minutes.

Minced Lamb Keema

Minced Lamb Keema

You will need:

- 2 tbsp oil
- 1 medium onion, chopped
- 1 tsp garlic, peeled and finely grated
- 1 tsp fresh ginger, grated
- 1 tsp turmeric
- 1 tsp salt
- 2–3 fresh green chillies, chopped
- 150 g (5 oz) tinned tomatoes
- 600 g (1 lb, 5 oz) lamb mince
- 1 tbsp Worcestershire sauce
- 150 g (5 oz) peas
- 1 tsp garam masala
- fresh coriander to garnish

Preparation time: 5–10 minutes
Cooking time: 40–45 minutes
Serves: 4

1. Heat the oil in a medium-sized pan. Sauté the finely chopped onions until golden brown, stirring occasionally. Add garlic and ginger and stir-fry for a further 2–3 minutes.

2. Add the turmeric, salt, fresh chillies and tomatoes and cook for 2–3 minutes.

3. Add the minced lamb and Worcestershire sauce to the pan and mix together with the spice mixture. Cook for 30–40 minutes on a medium heat, stirring occasionally.

4. Add the peas and the garam masala and cook for a further five minutes.

5. Serve garnished with fresh coriander.

Lamb In Spinach

Lamb In Spinach

You will need:

- 600 g (1 lb, 5 oz) lean lamb
- 2 tbsp of ghee/oil
- 2 medium onions chopped
- 1 tsp fresh ginger, finely grated
- 1 tsp fresh garlic, peeled and grated
- 100 g (3½ oz) tomatoes
- 1 green chilli, chopped
- ½ tsp of turmeric
- 1 tsp salt
- 1 kg (2 lb, 3 oz) tinned, frozen or fresh, trimmed and washed spinach
- 300 ml (10½ fl.oz) water

Preparation time: 10–15 minutes
Cooking time: 1 hour 50 minutes
Serves: 4

1. Trim the lamb and cut into bite-size pieces. Heat the ghee / oil in a medium-sized pan.

2. Sauté the onions, ginger and garlic for 2–3 minutes, then add the lamb pieces. Cover and cook for ten minutes on a low heat, stirring occasionally. Remove the lid and cook for a further ten minutes.

3. Add the tomatoes, chilli, turmeric and salt to the mixture and stir-fry for 3–4 minutes.

4. Add 200 ml of the water, cover and cook for 35–40 minutes.

5. Add the spinach and the rest of the water and cook for a further 45–55 minutes on a low heat. If the lamb is not tender then increase the heat slightly and cook uncovered until the surplus liquid has been absorbed, then cook for a further 8–10 minutes.

6. Serve with rice or naan (page 64).

Lamb Kebabs

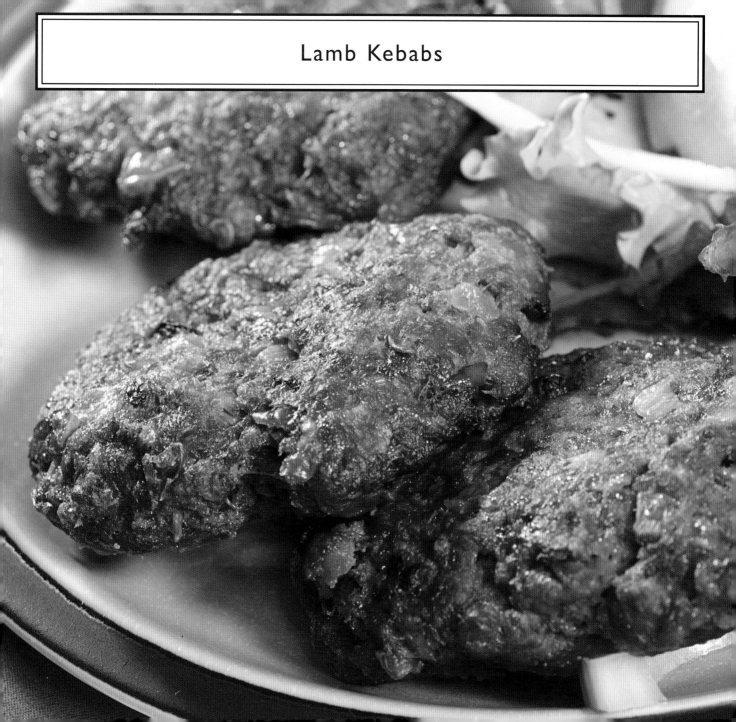

Lamb Kebabs

You will need:
- 450 g (1 lb) minced lamb
- breadcrumbs from one slice of bread
- 1 tsp garlic, peeled and finely grated
- 1 tsp garam masala
- 1 tsp ginger, finely grated
- 2 fresh green chillies, chopped
- 1 medium onion, finely chopped
- 1 tbsp soy sauce
- ½ tsp turmeric
- 1 tbsp of lemon juice
- ½ bunch fresh coriander

Preparation time: 10 minutes
Cooking time: 15–20 minutes
Serves: 4

1. Place all of the ingredients in a large mixing bowl. Mix together and knead into a ball.

2. Divide the mixture into eight patties or eight kebab shapes.

3. Cook under a grill on a medium heat for 8–10 minutes until each side has browned. Turn over halfway through cooking. Alternatively, cook over a hot barbeque on skewers.

4. Serve with a side salad.

Tip: *You can use half an egg to bind the mixture rather than breadcrumbs if you prefer.*

Fish Pakora

Fish Pakora

You will need:

- 550 g (1 lb 3 oz) cod fillets
- 1 tbsp lemon juice
- 200 g (7 oz) gram flour
- ½ bunch of fresh coriander, chopped
- 1 fresh green chilli, chopped
- 1 tsp salt
- ½ tsp turmeric
- 200 ml (7 fl oz) water
- 450 ml (16 fl oz) oil
- lemon wedges, lettuce leaves

Preparation time: 5–10 minutes
Cooking time: 10–15 minutes
Marinating time: 15 minutes
Serves: 3–4

1. Cut the cod fillets into bite size pieces and marinate with the lemon juice for a few minutes.

2. Place the gram flour, fresh coriander, chilli, salt and turmeric in a mixing bowl and mix together.

3. Add the water to the gram flour mixture until the mixture is of the consistency of a batter. Coat the marinated fish pieces in the batter. Leave to marinate for 15 minutes.

4. Place the oil in a pan to deep fry the fish (oil should be on a medium heat). Fry the fish until golden brown – approximately five minutes.

5. Once the fish is cooked, lift out of the oil with a perforated metal spoon and pat off any excess oil with kitchen towel.

6. Serve the pakoras on a bed of lettuce with lemon wedges.

Fish Curry

Fish Curry

You will need:

- 1 tsp mustard seeds
- 1 tsp white cumin seeds
- 3–4 tbsp oil
- 550 g (1 lb 3 oz) skinless cod fillets
- 1 medium onion, finely sliced
- 1 ½ tsp ginger, finely grated
- 1 ½ tsp of fresh garlic, peeled and finely grated
- 150 g (5 oz) tinned tomatoes
- 1 fresh tomato, diced
- 1 tsp salt
- 1 tsp chilli powder
- ½ tsp turmeric
- 200 ml (7 fl oz) coconut milk
- fresh coriander, to garnish

Preparation time: 10–12 minutes
Cooking time: 15–20 minutes
Serves: 4

1. Grind the mustard seeds and white cumin seeds in a pestle and mortar.

2. Heat half the oil in a large frying pan and cook the fish for one minute each side, so it is sealed.

3. Heat the remaining oil in a kahari or large heavy-based pan and add the mustard seeds and white cumin seeds. Stir-fry for 30 seconds. Add the onion and sauté on a medium heat until golden brown.

4. Add the ginger, garlic and stir-fry for three minutes. Add the tinned tomatoes and fresh tomato, salt, chilli powder, turmeric and cook for a further 3–5 minutes. Add the coconut milk and cook for a further 2–5 minutes.

5. Carefully add the fish and cover with the sauce. Simmer for one minute. Garnish with fresh coriander.

Prawn Curry

Prawn Curry

You will need:

- 1 tsp white cumin seeds
- 2 tbsp oil
- 2 bay leaves
- 1 small onion, finely chopped
- 1 tsp garlic, finely grated
- 1 tsp ginger, finely grated
- ½ tsp turmeric
- 1 fresh green chilli, chopped
- 1 tsp salt
- ½ tsp black peppercorns
- 100 g (3 ½ oz) tinned tomatoes
- 250 g (9 oz) raw king prawns
- ½ tsp garam masala
- 150 ml (5 fl.oz) double cream

Preparation time: 8–10 minutes
Cooking time: 20 minutes
Serves: 4

1. Grind the white cumin seeds in a pestle and mortar. Heat the oil in a saucepan and stir-fry the white cumin seeds and bay leaves for a few seconds.

2. Add the chopped onion, garlic and ginger and sauté until the onions are golden brown.

3. Add the turmeric, fresh chilli, salt, black peppercorns and tinned tomatoes and cook for five minutes.

4. Stir the prawns and garam masala into the mixture and cook for 3–4 minutes. Take the pan off the heat to stir in the cream and then return to the heat and cook for a further 2–3 minutes. Leave the dish to stand for 1–2 minutes before serving. Serve on a bed of rice.

Mixed Vegetable Curry

Mixed Vegetable Curry

You will need:

- 3 tbsp ghee / oil
- I tsp black mustard seeds
- I tsp white cumin seeds
- 3 or 4 curry leaves
- I medium sized onion, chopped
- I tsp garlic, peeled and finely grated
- I tsp ginger, finely grated
- I fresh tomato
- 100 g (3 ½ oz) tinned tomatoes
- I tsp chilli powder
- ½ tsp turmeric
- I tsp salt
- 2 medium potatoes, diced
- ½ medium cauliflower, diced
- 200 g (7 oz) frozen or fresh peas
- 200 g (7 oz) frozen mixed vegetables
- 300 ml (10 ½ fl.oz) water
- I tbsp lemon juice
- I tsp garam masala
- fresh coriander to garnish (optional)

Preparation time: 10–15 minutes
Cooking time: 35 minutes
Serves: 4

1. Heat the ghee / oil in a saucepan. Grind the mustard and cumin seeds in a pestle and mortar then add to the pan. Add curry leaves and stir-fry for ten seconds until they turn a shade darker.

2. Add the onion, garlic and ginger and sauté gently until the onions are golden brown.

3. Add the fresh and tinned tomatoes, chilli powder, turmeric and salt and stir well. Cook for three minutes.

4. Add the potatoes, cauliflower, peas and frozen mixed vegetables and stir-fry for five minutes.

5. Add the water, cover and leave to simmer on a medium heat for 10–12 minutes, stirring occasionally. The vegetables should be tender. If they are not, cook for a further 3–4 minutes, adding more water if necessary.

6. Add the lemon juice and garam masala to the pan. Cover and leave to simmer for a further 2–3 minutes, stirring occasionally.

7. Turn off the heat once the vegetables are cooked and leave for 2–3 minutes before serving. Transfer to a plate and garnish with fresh coriander.

Spinach and Cheese (Palak/Saag Paneer)

Spinach and Cheese (Palak/Saag Paneer)

You will need:

- 4 tbsp cooking oil
- 300 g (10 ½ oz) paneer (see recipe p.9)
- 2 tbsp ghee/oil
- 2 medium onions, finely chopped
- 1 tsp garlic, peeled and finely grated
- 1 tsp ginger, finely grated
- 2 fresh green chillies, chopped
- 1 tsp tomato purée
- 1 tsp salt
- 500 g (17 ½ oz) tinned, frozen, or trimmed, washed, fresh spinach
- 1 tsp garam masala

Preparation time: 10–15 minutes
Cooking time: 40–45 minutes
Serves: 4

1. Heat the oil in a frying pan and stir-fry the paneer on all sides until golden brown.

2. Heat the ghee/oil in a saucepan. Sauté the onions, garlic and ginger until the onions are golden brown.

3. Add the chillies, tomato purée and salt and stir-fry for 3–5 minutes.

4. Add the spinach and cook, stirring occasionally, for 20–25 minutes.

5. Add the garam masala and cook for a further 3–4 minutes.

6. Add the cooked paneer to the pan and stir in the mixture for 2–3 minutes.

7. Serve with hot pooris (p.65), roti (p.67) or plain rice (p.57).

Okra Curry (Bindia – Ladies' Fingers)

Okra Curry (Bindia – Ladies' Fingers)

You will need:

- 450 g (1 lb) okra (ladies fingers)
- 2 tbsp oil
- 2 medium onions, sliced
- 1 tsp chilli powder or 1 fresh green chilli, chopped
- 1 tsp salt
- ½ tsp turmeric
- 1 tbsp lemon juice
- ½ tsp garam masala
- fresh coriander to garnish (optional)

Preparation time: 5–10 minutes
Cooking time: 20–25 minutes
Serves: 4

1. Rinse, drain and pat the okra dry. Use a sharp knife to remove the ends and cut into 2.5 cm (1 in.) pieces.

2. Heat the oil in a large frying pan. Sauté the onions for 2 minutes.

3. Add the chilli powder, salt and turmeric and cook for one minute. Add the okra and cook on a low heat, stirring occasionally, for 10–15 minutes until the okra is tender.

4. Drizzle the lemon juice and garam masala over the mixture and leave to simmer for one minute. Garnish with coriander if desired.

Pumpkin Curry

Pumpkin Curry

You will need:

- 2–3 tbsp ghee/oil
- 1 tsp white cumin seeds
- 1 large onion, finely chopped
- 1 tsp mango powder
- 1 tsp fresh ginger, grated
- 1 tsp fresh garlic, peeled and grated
- 1 tsp chilli powder
- 1 tbsp tomato purée
- 2 tbsp lemon juice
- ½ tsp turmeric
- 1 tsp sugar
- 1 tsp salt
- 450 g (1 lb) orange or green pumpkin, cubed
- 200 ml (7 fl.oz) water
- 200 ml (7 fl.oz) double cream
- ½ tsp garam masala

Preparation time: 10–12 minutes
Cooking time: 30 minutes
Serves: 4

1. Heat the ghee/oil in a large frying pan. Grind the cumin seeds in a pestle and mortar, then stir-fry for 30 seconds. Add the onion and cook until golden brown.

2. Add the mango powder, ginger, garlic, chilli powder, tomato purée, lemon juice, turmeric, sugar and salt to the pan and mix together. Stir-fry for 2–3 minutes.

3. Add the cubed pumpkin and stir-fry for 4–5 minutes on a medium-low heat.

4. Add the water, cover and cook over a low heat for 10–15 minutes stirring occasionally until the pumpkin is tender.

5. Add the cream and garam masala and simmer until the pumpkin is soft. Serve with gram flour bread (p.69) or chapati/roti (p.67).

Bombay Potatoes

Bombay Potatoes

You will need:
- 500 g (17 ½ oz) potatoes
- 2 tbsp ghee/oil
- 1 tsp cumin seeds
- 1 tsp black mustard seeds
- 1 tsp garlic, peeled and finely grated
- 1 tsp fresh ginger, grated
- 2 fresh green chillies, chopped
- ½ tsp turmeric
- 1 tsp salt
- 100 g (3 ½ oz) tinned tomatoes or 3 large tomatoes
- 150 ml (5 fl.oz) water
- 1 tsp garam masala
- fresh coriander to garnish

Preparation time: 10–12 minutes
Cooking time: 30 minutes
Serves: 4

1. Clean and rinse the potatoes and cut into cubes.

2. Heat the ghee/oil in a saucepan and stir-fry the cumin and mustard seeds on a medium heat for five seconds.

3. Add the garlic, ginger, chillies, turmeric, salt and tomatoes and stir-fry for 1–2 minutes on a medium heat.

4. Place the potatoes in the pan and coat in the mixture. Add the water and cook the potatoes for 10–15 minutes until the potatoes are tender.

If the potatoes are not cooked after 15 minutes then add another 150 ml (5 fl.oz) of water and leave to simmer for a further 10 minutes.

5. Once the potatoes are cooked add the garam masala and cook for a further 2–3 minutes.

6. Garnish with fresh coriander and serve with pooris (p. 65).

Kidney Bean Curry

You will need:
- 2 tbsp ghee/oil
- 1 small onion, finely chopped
- 1 ½ tsp garlic, peeled and finely grated
- 1 ½ tsp ginger, finely grated
- 1 tsp ground coriander
- 1 tsp ground cumin
- 2 tsp salt
- 2 tbsp lemon juice
- ½ tsp turmeric
- 100 g (3 ½ oz) tinned tomatoes
- 500 g (17 ½ oz) tinned kidney beans, drained and rinsed
- 1 tsp garam masala
- fresh coriander to garnish (optional)

Preparation time: 8–10 minutes
Cooking time: 30–35 minutes or 1 hour 40 minutes if using dried, soaked beans
Serves: 4

1. Heat the ghee/oil in a saucepan and sauté the onions, garlic and ginger for approximately ten minutes until the onions are golden brown.

2. Add the ground coriander, cumin, salt, lemon juice and turmeric, then the tomatoes and cook for another five minutes.

3. Add the beans and their cooking liquid; if prepared from dried beans, simmer uncovered until the beans are soft. Add the garam masala and cook for a further minute. Then turn off the heat and garnish with fresh coriander if desired.

Note: *You can use dried kidney beans. Soak the beans overnight in water and cover. Drain, cover with 300 ml (10 ½ fl.oz) fresh water and bring to the boil. Add one teaspoon of salt and simmer for about 50–60 minutes, until the beans are tender.*

Mushroom, Pepper, Tomato and Onion Curry

Mushroom, Pepper, Tomato and Onion Curry

You will need:
- 2 tbsp ghee / oil
- 1 tsp white cumin seeds
- 1 tsp black mustard seeds
- 1 fresh green chilli, chopped
- 1 tsp garlic, peeled and finely grated
- 1 tsp ginger, finely grated
- 1 medium onion, sliced
- 200 g (7 oz) mushrooms, sliced
- 3 fresh tomatoes, sliced
- 1 red pepper, sliced
- 1 yellow pepper, sliced
- ½ tsp turmeric
- ½–1 tsp salt
- 1 tsp garam masala
- 1 tbsp of lemon juice
- fresh coriander to garnish

Preparation time: 10–15 minutes
Cooking time: 25–30 minutes
Serves: 4

1. Heat the ghee / oil in a large frying pan. Grind the cumin seeds and mustard seeds in a pestle and mortar and stir-fry for 30 seconds.

2. Add the green chilli. garlic, ginger and onion and cook until the onions are golden brown.

3. Place the mushrooms, tomatoes, peppers, turmeric and salt in the pan and cook for 5–10 minutes, or until soft.

4. Add the garam masala and lemon juice and cook for a further three minutes.

5. Garnish with coriander and serve.

Potato and Aubergine Curry (Aloo Bhutoun)

Potato and Aubergine Curry (Aloo Bhutoun)

You will need:

- 450 g (1 lb) small aubergines
- 1 ½ tsp salt
- 1 tsp mango powder
- 1 tsp garam masala
- 1 tbsp oil
- 1 medium onion, finely sliced
- 1 ½ tsp ginger, finely grated
- 1 ½ tsp of fresh garlic, peeled and finely grated
- 1 fresh tomato, diced
- 150 g (5 oz) tinned tomatoes
- 1–2 fresh green chillies, chopped
- ½ tsp turmeric
- 400 g (14 oz) potatoes, peeled and diced

Preparation time: 10–15 minutes
Cooking time: 40–45 minutes
Serves: 4

1. Wash the small aubergines and slit into quarters – do not cut all the way through.

2. Mix together half to one teaspoon of the salt, the mango powder and the garam masala. Stuff the small aubergines with this mixture.

3. Heat the oil in a pan. Sauté the onion until golden brown. Add the ginger and garlic and stir-fry for 2–3 minutes. Add the fresh and tinned tomatoes, the remaining salt, the chillies and the turmeric and cook for a further 3–4 minutes.

4. Add the potatoes, stir well and cook for five minutes. Add the aubergines and cook for 15–20 minutes until the potatoes are tender.

Note: *If small aubergines are unavailable then you can use large aubergines.*

Blackeye Bean Curry

Blackeye Bean Curry

You will need:

- 400 g (14 oz) blackeye beans
- 300 ml (10 ½ fl.oz) water
- 1 ½ tsp salt
- 2 tbsp ghee / oil
- 1 small onion, finely chopped
- 1 tsp garlic, peeled and finely grated
- 1 ½ tsp ginger, finely grated
- 1 tsp ground coriander
- 1 tsp ground cumin
- 2 tbsp lemon juice
- ½ tsp turmeric
- 150 g (5 oz) tinned tomatoes
- ½ tsp garam masala
- fresh coriander

Preparation time: Soak beans overnight, plus
8–10 minutes
Cooking time: 1 hour 30 minutes
Serves: 6

1. Soak the beans overnight, covered. Drain, cover with the water and bring to the boil. Add a teaspoon of the salt and simmer for about 45 minutes, until the beans are tender.

2. Heat the ghee / oil in a saucepan and sauté the onions, garlic and ginger for approximately 5–10 minutes until the onions are golden brown.

3. Add the remaining salt, the ground coriander, cumin, lemon juice, turmeric and tomatoes and cook for another five minutes. Add the beans and their cooking liquid.

4. Simmer, uncovered, until the beans are soft. Add the garam masala and garnish with fresh coriander.

Note: *You can use tinned blackeye beans. Drain and rinse them and follow the recipe from step 2.*

White Chickpea Curry (Chitai Sholay)

White Chickpea Curry (Chitai Sholay)

You will need:
- 400 g (14 oz) white chickpeas (tinned chickpeas can be used)
- 425 ml (15 fl.oz) water
- 2 tsp salt
- 2 tbsp ghee/oil
- 1 black cardamom or 3 green cardamom
- 1 tsp coriander seeds
- 1 cinnamon stick
- 1 medium onion, finely chopped
- 1 tsp garlic, peeled and finely grated or chopped
- 1 tsp ginger, finely grated or chopped
- 150 g (5 oz) tinned tomatoes
- 1 tsp chilli powder
- 1 tsp chana masala
- 1 tbsp lemon juice
- 1 tsp garam masala

Preparation time: Soak dry peas overnight, plus 10–12 minutes
Cooking time: 1 hour 40 minutes or 30–40 minutes if using tinned chickpeas
Serves: 4

1. Wash and soak the white chickpeas in a generous amount of water overnight. Drain and place with the water and one teaspoon of the salt in a saucepan and boil until the chickpeas are soft. If using dry chickpeas boil for 50 minutes–1 hour until the chickpeas are tender.

2. Heat the ghee/oil in a saucepan. Grind the cardamom, coriander seeds and cinnamon stick in a pestle and mortar or electric grinder. Stir-fry for 10 seconds.

3. Add the chopped onion and sauté until golden brown. Then add the garlic and ginger and cook for 2–3 minutes.

4. Add the tinned tomatoes, chilli powder and remaining salt and cook for 3–4 minutes. Add the chickpeas, water and the chana masala. Gently stir together and cook for 20–30 minutes. Drizzle with lemon juice then add the garam masala. (If using tinned chickpeas you only need to cook for 10–12 minutes and begin at step 2.)

5. Serve with plain boiled rice (p.57) or pooris (p.65).

Note: *You can make black (kala) chickpea curry in the same way substituting black chickpeas in place of white chickpeas.*

Spinach and Chickpea Lentils (Saag and Chana Daal)

Spinach and Chickpea Lentils (Saag and Chana Daal)

You will need:

- 225 g (8 oz) dried chickpea lentils (Chana Daal)
- 850 ml (30 fl.oz) water
- 2–3 tbsp ghee / oil
- 1 tsp white cumin seeds
- 1 tsp black mustard seeds
- 1 medium onion, chopped
- 1 tsp garlic, peeled and finely grated
- 1 tsp ginger, finely grated
- 1 tsp salt
- 1 fresh green chilli, chopped
- 400 g (14 oz) tinned, frozen or fresh spinach, trimmed and washed
- ½ tsp garam masala
- 2 tbsp lemon juice

Preparation time: Soak dry beans overnight, plus
10–15 minutes
Cooking time: 1 hour 20 minutes
Serves: 4

1. Wash and soak the chickpea lentils overnight in a generous amount of water. Drain, then place in a pan with the water, cover, and boil for 30–40 minutes. Strain the chickpea lentils and leave aside. Keep the stock for use later.

2. Heat the ghee / oil in a saucepan. Grind the cumin and mustard seeds in a pestle and mortar or electric mixer. Stir-fry for 30 seconds. Add the onion and sauté until golden brown. Add the garlic, ginger, salt and green chilli. Reduce the heat and stir-fry for 4–5 minutes.

3. Add the spinach and mix well. Cook for 20–25 minutes. Add the cooked lentils and stir together. Cook for a further 10–20 minutes and add the garam masala.

4. Lastly drizzle lemon juice over the dish.

Dry Lentils (Urid Daal)

Dry Lentils (Urid Daal)

You will need:

- 225 g (8 oz) urid lentils
- 1.2 litres (2 pts) water
- 1 tsp salt
- ½ tsp turmeric
- 2 tbsp ghee / oil
- 1 medium onion, chopped
- 1 tsp garlic, peeled and finely grated
- 1 tsp ginger, finely grated
- 1 fresh green chilli, chopped
- 1 tbsp lemon juice
- 1 tsp garam masala

Preparation time: 5–10 minutes
Cooking time: 45 minutes
Serves: 2–4

1. Wash and rinse the lentils. Place in a saucepan with the water and bring to the boil. Add the salt and turmeric. Simmer for half an hour until the lentils are tender. Check the lentils are tender by rubbing them between your finger and thumb. Be careful not to overcook the lentils as they will split if they are overcooked. Strain and leave aside. Save the stock from the lentils for use later.

2. In a separate pan heat the ghee / oil. Add the onions, garlic, ginger and fresh chillies. Sauté until the onions are golden brown.

3. Add the drained cooked lentils to the onion mixture and stir. Add two tablespoons of the lentil stock and mix well. Cook on a medium to low heat until the water has evaporated then add the lemon juice and garam masala.

Plain Boiled Rice

Plain Boiled Rice

You will need:
- 1 tsp white cumin seeds (optional)
- 225 g (8 oz) basmati rice
- 425 ml (15 fl.oz) water
- ½ tsp salt

Preparation time: 5–8 minutes
Cooking time: 10–15 minutes
Serves: 4

1. Dust the pieces of steak very lightly in plain flour, while you grind the cumin seeds in a pestle and mortar. Then dry-fry in a pan for 30 seconds.

2. Wash and drain the rice. Place in a saucepan on a medium heat with the water, salt and cumin seeds. Bring to the boil and simmer for 10–15 minutes until the rice is tender. Drain and serve.

Pilau Rice

Pilau Rice

You will need:
- Pinch of saffron strands
- 2 tbsp hot water
- 225 g (8 oz) basmati rice
- 2 tbsp ghee / oil / butter
- 1 shallot or small onion, sliced
- 3 green cardamom pods
- 1 cinnamon stick
- 425 ml (15 fl.oz) water
- ½–1 tsp salt

Preparation time: 10 minutes
Cooking time: 10–15 minutes
Serves: 4

1. Grind the saffron in a pestle and mortar then place in a small bowl with the hot water and set aside for 5–10 minutes. Then remove the saffron strands.

2. Rinse and drain the rice twice in a sieve.

3. Melt the ghee / oil / butter in a saucepan and sauté the shallot for two minutes. Add the cardamom pods, cinnamon and rice and mix well.

4. Add the water, the saffron mixture and the salt. Bring to the boil on a medium heat then reduce the heat, cover the pan and simmer for 10–15 minutes until the rice has absorbed all the water. Remove the cinnamon stick before serving.

Mushroom Fried Rice

Mushroom Fried Rice

You will need:

- 225 g (8 oz) basmati rice
- 425 ml (15 fl.oz) water
- 2 tbsp oil
- 1 tsp white cumin seeds
- 3 curry leaves
- 250 g (9 oz) mushrooms, chopped
- pinch of salt
- ½ tsp of turmeric

Preparation time: 5-8 minutes
Cooking time: 10–15 minutes
Serves: 4

1. Rinse the rice and boil in the water until cooked.
   Set aside to cool.

2. Heat the oil in a pan and stir fry the cumin seeds and
   curry leaves for 30 seconds. Add the mushrooms, salt,
   turmeric and the cooked rice and stir until well
   combined for five minutes. Serve.

Naan Bread

Naan Bread

You will need:

- 1 tsp sugar
- 1 tsp fresh yeast
- 150 ml (5 fl.oz) warm water
- 200 g (7 oz) plain flour
- 50 g (2 oz) ghee / oil
- 1 tsp salt
- 1 tbsp butter for grilling
- 1 tsp poppy seeds

Preparation time: 1 hour 45 minutes
Cooking time: 20 minutes
Serves: 4

1. Place the sugar and the yeast in a small bowl with the warm water. Mix together until the yeast has dissolved. Leave aside for 10 minutes until the mixture is frothy.

2. Place the flour in a large mixing bowl. Make a well in the middle of the flour and gradually add the ghee / oil, salt and yeast mixture. Mix together using your hands or place in a food processor to form a soft dough. Add a little more water if the dough is too dry.

3. Place the dough on a floured surface and knead for 5 minutes until smooth. Return to the bowl, cover and leave to rise in a warm place for 1 ½ hours until it has doubled in size.

4. Turn the dough out on a floured surface and knead for 2–3 minutes. Divide into small balls and roll out to a circle of 12 cm (5 in.) diameter and 1 cm (½ in.) thick. Place onto a greased sheet of foil and cook under a very hot grill for 5–10 minutes. Turn twice and brush each side with butter.

5. Once cooked, sprinkle with poppy seeds and serve straight away.

Pooris

Pooris

You will need:
- 225 g (8 oz) chapati flour
- ½ tsp salt
- 150 ml (5 fl.oz) water
- 600 ml (21 fl.oz) oil
- 75 g (2 ½ oz) chapati flour for rolling

Preparation time: 10 minutes
Cooking time: 10–20 minutes
Makes: 10

1. Mix the flour and salt together in a bowl. Make a well in the centre of the flour. Gradually pour in the water and mix together to form a soft dough, adding more water if necessary. Knead until smooth and leave aside in a warm place for 15 minutes, then divide into 10 small balls.

2. Heat the oil in a deep frying pan on a high heat. Once hot, turn down to a medium heat.

3. On a lightly floured surface, roll out the balls individually to form a thin circular shape of 10–12 cm (4–5 in.) diameter.

4. Deep-fry in batches for 30 seconds to one minute on each side until golden brown (pooris do not need to be cooked for long if the oil is hot). The pooris should puff up. Remove from the pan and drain on kitchen towel. Serve immediately or wrap in foil to be reheated later.

Chapati / Roti

Chapati / Roti

You will need:
- 225 g (8 oz) wholemeal chapati (ata) flour
- 200 ml (7 fl oz) water
- 75 g (2 ½ oz) chapati flour for rolling

Preparation time: 10–15 minutes
Cooking time: 15 minutes
Serves: 10–12

1. Place the flour in a large mixing bowl. Make a well in the centre and gradually pour in the water mixing with your hands to form a soft dough.

2. Knead for 6–8 minutes, leave aside for 10 minutes and then divide into 10–12 small balls.

3. Roll out the balls on a floured surface to a circle of 12–15 cm (5–6 in.). Shake off any excess flour before cooking.

4. Place a heavy-based frying pan on a high heat. Once the pan is hot, reduce the heat to a medium setting.

5. Place the chapati / roti, one by one, into the dry pan and cook on one side for 15-20 seconds until it starts to brown slightly and bubble, then turn over. Press down on the chapati with a clean tea towel to cook it evenly for 1–2 minutes, then turn it over and cook the other side again for 30 seconds to one minute until lightly browned. Turn the chapati over again and finish cooking the other side for 1–2 minutes until lightly brown.

Gram Flour Bread

Gram Flour Bread

You will need:
- 100 g (3 ½ oz) chapati (ata) flour
- 75 g (3 oz) gram flour
- ½ tsp salt
- 1 small onion, finely chopped
- ½ bunch of fresh coriander, chopped
- 2 fresh green chillies, chopped and de-seeded if preferred
- 150 ml (5 fl.oz) water
- 2 tsp ghee/oil

Preparation time: 15 minutes
Cooking time: 15 minutes
Serves: 4

1. Mix together the chapati flour, gram flour and salt in a large mixing bowl.

2. Add the onion, fresh coriander and chillies to the bowl and mix together.

3. Make a well in the flour and gradually add the water and mix to form a soft dough. Cover the dough with a damp tea towel and set aside for 15 minutes.

4. Knead the dough for 6–8 minutes and divide into 6–8 equal portions. Roll out the portions on a floured surface to a circle of approximately 15–17 cm (6–7 in.).

5. Heat a heavy-based frying pan on a high heat. Once hot, reduce the heat to medium. Individually cook each portion for 1 ½ minutes, turning over 2–3 times while cooking, brushing each side with ghee / oil as you turn.

Plain Fried Layered Bread (Parantha)

Plain Fried Layered Bread (Parantha)

You will need:
- 225 g (8 oz) chapati (ata) flour
- ½ tsp salt
- 200 ml (7 fl.oz) water
- 60 g (2 oz) butter (divided equally per parantha, see step 2)
- 2 tbsp ghee / oil

Preparation time: 10–15 minutes
Cooking time: 15–20 minutes
Serves: 6–8

1. Place the flour in a mixing bowl. Make a well in the flour, add the salt, then gradually add the water and mix to form a smooth dough. Leave aside for 5–10 minutes, then divide into 6–8 small ball shapes.

2. Roll out each portion to a circle of approximately 10 cm (4 in.). Then divide the butter and place a knob in the middle of each portion.

3. Fold the left, right, top and bottom sides inwards to encase the butter, creating a square shape. Roll these out again to approximately 12 cm (5 in.) square.

4. Heat a heavy-based frying pan on a high heat then, once hot, reduce the heat to medium. Cook the parantha individually, cooking each side briefly for 30 seconds to a minute then brush with ghee / oil and cook for a further 2–3 minutes. Both sides should be a light brown. Serve with yoghurt.

Onion Bhaji

Onion Bhaji

You will need:

- 2 medium onions, finely sliced
- 1 tbsp gram flour
- 1 tsp mango powder
- ½–1 tsp chilli powder
- ½–1 tsp salt
- 2 tsp chaat masala
- 600 ml (21 fl.oz) vegetable or sunflower oil

Note: *You can substitute the onions with 250 g (9 oz) chopped mushrooms/potatoes or any other vegetables for variation. You can also adjust the seasonings according to taste.*

Preparation time: 5–10 minutes
Cooking time: 10–15 minutes
Serves: 3–4

1. Place all of the ingredients, apart from the oil, in a mixing bowl. Mix together with your hands and form small balls with the mixture.

2. Pour the oil into a wok and heat on a high heat. Once hot reduce the heat to medium. The oil should be hot enough that a small piece of the mixture should sizzle.

3. Use a metal, slotted spoon to place the balls into the hot oil and deep fry in batches for 2–3 minutes or until golden brown, turning over while cooking. Remove from the oil and drain on kitchen towel.

Aloo Tikka

Aloo Tikka

You will need:
- 500 g (18 oz) potatoes, boiled, peeled and mashed
- 1 tsp cumin powder
- 1 tbsp cornflour
- ½–1 tsp chilli powder
- ½ bunch fresh coriander
- ½–1 tsp salt to taste
- juice of ½ a lemon
- 1 fresh green chilli, chopped (optional)
- 1 tsp garam masala
- 6–7 tbsp vegetable / sunflower oil for frying

Preparation time: 15 minutes
Cooking time: 15 minutes
Serves: 2–3

1. Mix all the ingredients together in a mixing bowl, except the oil.

2. Divide into six equal portions and roll them into balls. Flatten each ball between the palms into patties.

3. Heat the oil in a frying pan and shallow fry the patties over a medium heat until golden brown and crisp on both sides. Drain and pat dry on a kitchen towel. Serve hot with a side salad and tamarind chutney.

Raita – Onion, Cucumber and Mint

Raita – Onion, Cucumber and Mint

Preparation time: 5–10 minutes
Serves: 3–4

Onion Raita:
- 1 onion, finely chopped
- 200 ml (7 fl.oz) yoghurt
- 4 tbsp water (optional)
- ½ tsp salt
- 2–3 mint leaves to garnish

1. Place all the ingredients, except the mint leaves, in a bowl and mix together. Transfer to a serving bowl and garnish with the mint leaves.

Cucumber Raita:
- 225 g (8 oz) cucumber
- 1 medium onion, finely chopped
- ½ tsp salt
- ½ tsp fresh mint
- 200 ml (7 fl.oz) yoghurt
- 4 tbsp water (optional)
- a slice of cucumber to garnish

1. Wash, peel and grate the cucumber. Place in a mixing bowl with the onion, salt and mint. Mix in the yoghurt and optional water and whip together with a spoon. Garnish with a slice of cucumber.

Mint Raita:
- 200 ml (7 fl.oz) yoghurt
- 4 tbsp water (optional)
- 1 small onion, chopped
- ½ tsp mint sauce
- ½ tsp salt
- fresh mint leaves to garnish

Note: *Only add water if the consistency of the yoghurt that you are using is too thick.*

1. Place the yoghurt in a bowl and add the water gradually, if necessary. Stir together with a spoon to form a smooth consistency.

2. Add the onion, mint sauce and salt. Stir together with a spoon. Transfer to a serving bowl and garnish with fresh mint leaves.

Fresh Green Mango Chutney

You will need:

- 500 g (18 oz) fresh, unripened, green mango
- 1 small onion, finely chopped
- ½ bunch coriander, chopped
- 1 tbsp sugar
- ½–1 tsp salt
- 1 tsp chilli powder
- 1 tsp ginger, finely grated
- 1 tsp garam masala

Preparation time: 5–8 minutes
Serves: 2–4

1. Wash, peel and dice the mango into small chunks then place in a blender. Add onion, fresh coriander, sugar, salt, chilli powder, ginger and garam masala and blend together for one minute, until the desired consistency is reached. Transfer to a serving bowl.

Tamarind Chutney

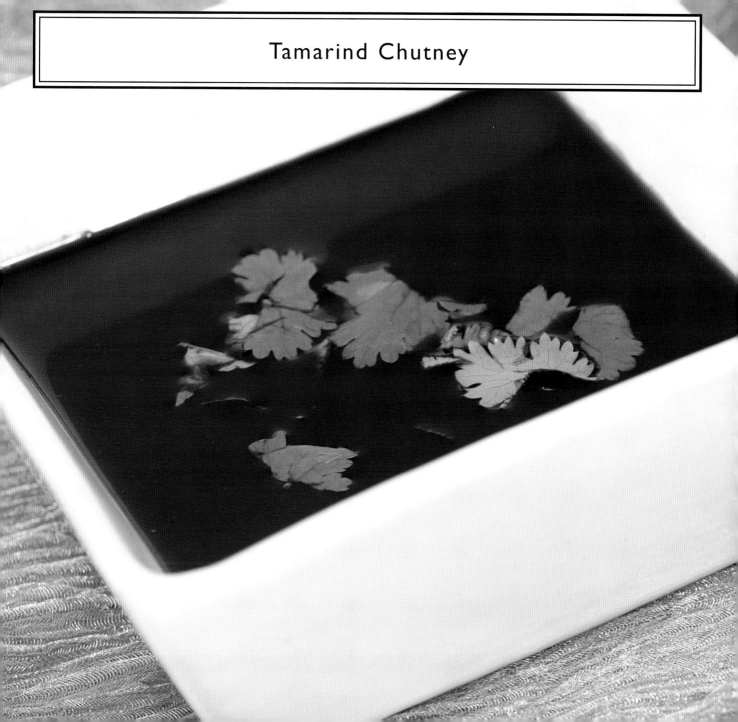

Tamarind Chutney

You will need:
- 2 tbsp tamarind paste
- 5 tbsp hot water
- 1 tsp chilli powder
- ½ tsp ground ginger
- ½ tsp salt
- 2–3 tsp sugar
- fresh coriander to garnish

Preparation time: 5 minutes
Serves: 4-6

1. Place the tamarind paste in a mixing bowl. Gradually add the hot water and mix together.

2. Add the chilli powder, ginger, salt and sugar to the mixture and stir well. Check seasonings and adjust according to taste.

3. Transfer to a serving dish and garnish with a few sprigs of fresh coriander.

Fresh Apple Chutney

Fresh Apple Chutney

You will need:

- 3–4 spring onions
- ½ bunch fresh coriander
- 1 medium cooking apple
- 1 tsp salt
- 1 tsp sugar
- coriander or apple, to garnish

Preparation time: 5–8 minutes
Serves: 4

1. Wash, dry and finely chop the spring onions and fresh coriander.

2. Wash the cooking apple, peel and chop it into small pieces and place in a blender with the chopped spring onions, coriander, salt and sugar.

3. Blend together for a few seconds until it forms a paste. Transfer to a small bowl and garnish with a few sprigs of fresh coriander or slices of apple.

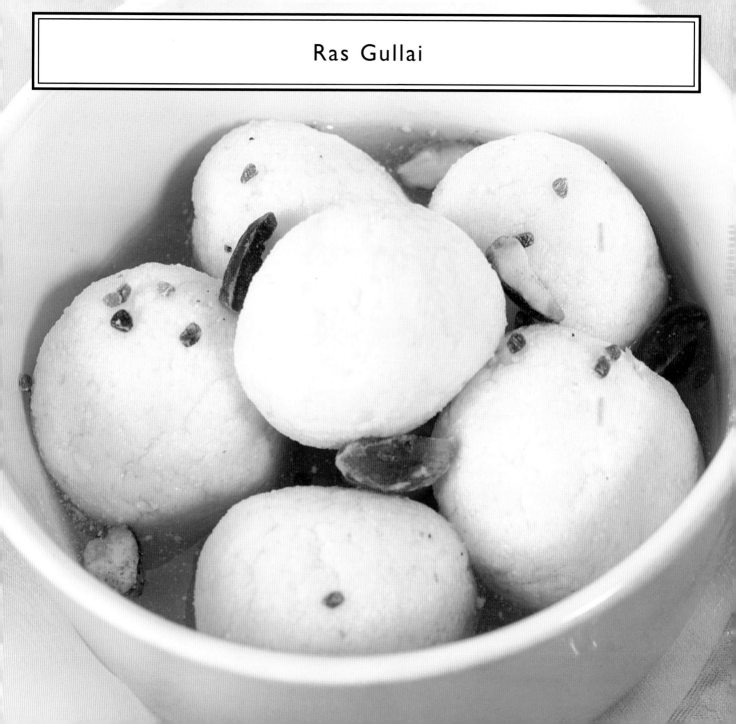

Ras Gullai

Ras Gullai

You will need:

- 1.7 litres (3 pts) full fat milk
- 2 tbsp white vinegar
- 1 tsp fine semolina
- 225 g (8 oz) sugar
- 850 ml (30 fl.oz) water
- 6–8 green cardamom pods, crushed
- pistachio nuts to garnish

Preparation time: 15–20 minutes
Cooking time: 1 hour 15 minutes
Serves: 14–16

1. Boil the milk in a saucepan and add the vinegar. When the milk curdles, sieve the milk so you are left with only the curd.

2. Add the semolina to the curd and knead either by hand or in a food mixer to form a smooth dough. Make about 10–12 small balls from the curd dough, 2 ½ cm (1 in.) in diameter.

3. Place the sugar, water and crushed cardamoms in a saucepan and boil for 15–20 minutes until it forms a light syrup. Place the small balls in the syrup once the sugar has dissolved. Gently mix and coat the balls in the syrup.

4. Simmer on a low heat for 30–45 minutes, stirring gently. Serve, garnished with pistachio nuts.

Note: *If you would prefer to make the ras gullai sweeter then add extra sugar to taste.*

Ras Malai

Ras Malai

You will need:
- 2.7 litres (6 pts) milk
- 3 tbsp white vinegar
- 1.2 litres (2 pts) water
- 180 g (6 ½ oz) sugar
- 6–8 green cardamom pods, crushed
- 1 tsp rosewater
- pistachio nuts, to garnish

Preparation time: 20–25 minutes
Cooking time: 1 hour 30 minutes
Makes: 12–15

1. Boil half the milk in a saucepan and add the vinegar. Once the milk curdles, sieve the milk so you are left with only the curd.

2. Knead the curd, either by hand or in a food mixer, to form a smooth dough. Make 12–15 small patties from the dough.

3. Heat the water, two tablespoons of the sugar and the crushed cardamom pods in a saucepan.

4. Place the patties in the water mixture and simmer for half an hour, then set aside.

5. Boil the remaining milk in a large saucepan, then reduce the heat and simmer until the milk has halved in quantity. Add the remaining sugar and stir until dissolved. Cook for 10–15 minutes, then add the rosewater.

6. Take the patties out of the water mixture and place in the pan with the milk mixture. Leave for an hour to cool, and serve garnished with pistachio nuts.

Gulab Jaman

Gulab Jaman

You will need:
- 600 g (1 lb, 6 oz) milk powder
- 200 g (7 oz) self-raising flour
- 1 tbsp fine semolina
- 1 tsp ghee / oil
- 700 ml (25 fl.oz) milk
- 600 ml (21 fl.oz) oil
- 450 g (1 lb) sugar
- 1.2 litres (42 fl.oz) water
- 6 green cardamom pods, crushed
- pistachio nuts, to garnish

Preparation time: 20–25 minutes
Cooking time: 45–50 minutes
Makes: 55–60

1. Mix the milk powder, flour, semolina and ghee / oil together then gradually add the milk until it forms a smooth dough.

2. Divide the dough into small balls approximately 2 ½ cm (1 in.) wide and set aside.

3. Heat the oil in a large pan or wok on a high heat. Once hot reduce the heat to medium-low. Deep fry the balls in batches until they are golden brown turning them over occasionally so they cook evenly. Remove from the oil with a slotted/perforated metal spoon and place on kitchen towel to remove any excess oil.

4. Place a separate saucepan on a gentle heat and boil the sugar, water and cardamom pods for 15–20 minutes, until it forms a light syrup. Remove from the heat.

5. Place the fried balls into the syrup and stir gently together. Put the pan back on the heat and simmer for a further 5-10 minutes, then take off the heat. Leave to stand for 10 minutes before serving. Garnish with pistachio nuts.

Note: *You can adjust the amount of sugar to taste.*

Sweet Rice With Saffron

Sweet Rice With Saffron

You will need:
- 1 pinch saffron
- 2 tbsp hot water
- 225 g (8 oz) basmati rice
- 1.2 litres (2 pts) water
- 225 g (8 oz) sugar
- 3 tbsp ghee / butter
- 3 green cardamom pods, crushed
- 3 cloves
- 25 g (1 oz) sultanas
- handful pistachio nuts
- handful flaked almonds

Preparation time: 10–15 minutes
Cooking time: 30 minutes
Serves: 4

1. Place the saffron in a small bowl with two tablespoons of hot water and leave aside for 5–8 minutes, then remove the saffron strands. The saffron should have coloured the water.

2. Rinse the rice twice and place in a saucepan with one litre (35 fl.oz) of the water and the saffron water. Bring to the boil, stirring occasionally. Once the rice is half cooked remove from the heat and strain. Set aside.

3. In a separate saucepan boil the sugar and the remaining 200 ml (7 fl.oz) water until the mixture forms a light syrup. Pour over the rice and mix well.

4. Heat the ghee / butter in another saucepan. Place the crushed cardamom pods, cloves, sultanas and pistachio nuts in the pan. Stir together for one minute. Pour the mixture over the rice and stir together. Leave the rice in the pan for 3–4 minutes, on a low heat, until the rice has absorbed the syrup. Garnish with almond flakes.

Lassi

Lassi

You will need:
- 425 g (15 oz) plain yoghurt
- 275–425 ml (10–15 fl.oz) water
- 1 tbsp sugar
- ½ cup crushed ice (optional)
- 1 tsp cardamom pods (optional)
- 1–2 tsp pistachio nuts (optional)

Preparation time: 3–5 minutes
Serves: 4

1. Place all the ingredients in a blender and blend together for a few minutes until frothy.

2. Pour into a tall glass and serve.

Note: *Add less or more water depending on the type of consistency you like.*

Glossary

Aloo	Potatoes
Adhrak	Ginger
Ata	Chapati flour
Bhutoun	Aubergines
Bindia	Okra
Badam	Almonds
Besan	Gram flour
Chite Sholay	white chickpeas
Dahi	yoghurt
Daal	lentils
Dalchini	cinnamon sticks
Dhaniya	fresh coriander
Garam masala	blend of cumin, black cardamom, coriander seeds, cinnamon and cloves
Ghee	clarified butter
Gram flour	a flour made from ground chickpeas
Haldi	turmeric
Jeera	cumin seeds

Karahi	Heavy-based Indian cooking pan
Korma	mild curry
Kala	black
Kali mirch sabat	black peppercorns
Lassi	popular yoghurt-based drink
Lachi	cardamom pods
Lasan	garlic
Masala	blend of spices
Mutter	peas
Methi	fenugreek
Oil	vegetable or olive or sunflower
Paneer	Indian cheese
Parantha	fried, layered bread
Pista	pistachio nuts
Roti	Indian bread
Rai	mustard seeds
Saag	spinach
Sholay	chickpeas

Tava	Heavy-based cooking pan for cooking roti/chapati
Vindaloo	hot curry

Conclusion

Hopefully you will enjoy trying out this range of recipes. The dishes are authentic and what any family from the Indian sub-continent might eat at home. As well as being tasty, they are easy to prepare and nutritious.

The choice of food from the Indian sub-continent is huge; there are so many different recipes to choose from it would be impossible to include them all in one book.

Many people in Asia follow a vegetarian diet so anybody wanting meat free dishes, can still enjoy spicy food. You will now be able to create some of the most famous and familiar dishes, such as vindaloo, korma and of course chicken tikka masala, which is one of the most popular dishes served in Indian restaurants today. You will also now be familiar with some less well-known dishes. They might look rather different from those ordered at a restaurant because there are no additives or artificial colourings used. (Red food colouring is often used to add extra colour in some restaurants.)

Whatever aspect of traditional Indian cuisine you are looking to make, you'll find examples in this book. So, happy cooking, and above all, have fun!